Father...
They Know Not What They Do!

God's Poetic Reach to a
Lost and Dying World.

By Vernon L. Coleman

Table of Contents

Introduction

This book is written for God's glory, to tell his story and a little bit of mine. My story is about having wonderful parents who raised me and my siblings, June and Van, to make wise choices in life and defraud no one. They put me in church at an early age to learn about Jesus, to follow him as they did.

I loved going to that little neighborhood Baptist church located on the next block from my home. I had friends there who wanted to learn more about Jesus, and we loved each other's company. Then slowly things changed. One by one my friends stopped attending. Then I saw some of the reasons why.

I saw and heard backbiting, bad behavior and hypocrisy in that church. It seemed like only a very few people there were living right except our beloved Sunday School teacher, Mr. Larry Taylor, Deacon and Mrs. Garrett, and a few others. The Pastor and congregation just seemed to ignore us young people. They built a basketball court inside an annex of the church and would seldom let us play there. We were not even teenagers yet. It was as though we did not exist.

Eventually all my friends left and so did I, but I did not want to leave God. I carried him in my heart and faithfully prayed to him every night. When it would thunder and lightning at night during a rainstorm, I thought God was talking to me. I still believe that is what occurred. I spoke back to him while the storm raged. We conversed as I lay in my bed unafraid.

The years rolled by and eventually this old world caught my eye. While it seemed in a way that God was always nearby, it appeared as though I was always trying to test how far away from God I could get.

Throughout my life, I seldom cursed. I never heard my parents swear, so that was a filthy habit I was never attracted to.

However other things I never saw them do, did attract me. I tried drugs, weed mostly, but not entirely. Alcohol, I could take it or leave it. Stealing was never my thing. I stole a pack of gum once out of a food store as a youngster. When my father discovered it, he whipped any attraction to stealing right out of me.

The ladies? Oh, the ladies. I knew how to sweet talk the ladies. Single, married, didn't matter. Black, White, Hispanic, did not matter, I loved the variety. It was like whatever woman I put on my radar to be mine became mine. I never looked like Denzel Washington, although I was not bad on the eyes either, I just seemed to know what words to say to women for them to lower their defenses. Once their defenses were down, full surrender.

Remember me telling you about how my dad whipped stealing out of me? Once, still living at home as a teenager, my mother caught me in my bedroom in bed with a married woman well out of her teenage years. To her credit, my mother did not open the door, she just banged on it telling me to get that woman out of her house. I had asked my sister, June, to warn me, which she did not, if she heard my mother returning home when I brought that woman to the house. Then I learned my sister must have had what is often called "selective amnesia". My mother, bless her heart, failed at the time to whip that sex attraction for the ladies out of me like my father whipped stealing out of me.

God long suffered with me. I knew church was not for me because I figured they all were like the one I had left as a youngster. Then one day, many years later, I heard my best buddy, my partner in using and selling drugs, my partner in crime, Terry, had got saved and that he was fearful of coming around me anymore because he did not want to lose his salvation. He didn't want to chase the ladies and use or sell drugs with me anymore.

I asked my friend, Steve, who related that news, "What is saved? What is that?" I had never heard of being saved or salvation.

Those words were never, ever even spoken at that little Baptist church I was going to as a youngster. The Baptist church speaks those terms now, some, but not then.

Sometime later me and my elusive friend, Terry, finally crossed paths. I asked him what was going on with him. He told me how he was at a party sitting in a chair. He said he was a little high but not real high. He said, suddenly, he heard a noise and looked and everyone that was in the room appeared to be a demon. He said that God spoke to him telling him he must change his life. He said he then dropped to his knees at that chair, amid the party, and cried out to God to forgive him of all his sins. He said when he arose from his knees, his "high" was gone. I was amazed at what he had just told me and somehow felt happy for him.

Many weeks went by and when I would see Terry, he was always trying to get me to go to church with him. Finally, out of curiosity and the desire to have Terry stop bugging me about it, I agreed.

That Sunday came and I went to his church. I forget if I met him there or rode with him. During that service, the people of that congregation were speaking in tongues, something I had heard about but never witnessed until that day. People were rolling on the floor, women had their dresses flying up, people were convulsing and foaming at the mouth and again, I heard a language I could not understand. I had no idea if they were praising God or cursing God. I told Terry, "I do not know what this is, but this ain't God!" I had that much sense to know that God received no glory in that. That service did not enlighten me. That service frightened me. I let Terry know, "Never again. Do not even bother inviting me to this place!"

Maybe a few months later, I saw Terry again and he told me that God told him to get out of that place. Terry told me that the only reason he went there was that a lady he used to date told him he should go there. Terry then said to me he had found another church, a church named the Church of God. He said

God had led him there. I told Terry, "Well you won't be leading me there."

I felt like I was ok, that I did not need to go to church. I was a student of that old teaching, "Do the best you can, and God will understand." I always thought that God had a real church but felt like finding it would be like finding a needle in a haystack. I was used to seeing people file out of different churches and then start smoking and swearing before they could hardly get out the door. I felt like I was on better footing with God than they were. I least I was not being a hypocrite. I knew I was having fun yet some things I wanted to stop but I could not. I felt like something was missing in my life. Sometimes I would feel lonely even when around my peers. Also, I was missing my friend, Terry. So eventually I agreed to come see his new church home.

I drove there one Sunday to meet him. I knew he was there, but I did not see him because it was a lot of people there unlike that other church that I had visited with him. A lot of the people there were young people, excited and smiling. Everyone there looked so clean-cut, decent, almost angelic. The choir sang like no other choir I had ever heard. No robes, no swaying, no stomping, just singing. They were singing praises to God in such a serene and beautiful way. I felt like I had almost walked into heaven compared to that previous church. There were no printed programs and even more remarkable they only passed the collection plate around ONE TIME! I figured in God's church there should be no need for begging. One time should do it. God will provide.

The Pastor, the late Elder Willie E. Gordon, preached straight from the Bible, no articles, no opinions, only "What thus saith the Lord." Pastor Gordon preached against sin, man-made religion, phony preachers and phony churches. He preached on how the ills of society and the troubles of mankind can be traced to sin.

He preached that sin separates man from God, that sin brings about heartache and hell. Pastor Gordon pulled the cover off the devil and exposed how the devil has deceived many people into thinking they will always have time to get things right with God and accept his only begotten son, Jesus Christ as their personal savior. Pastor Gordon preached on how the Bible says that Satan, seeks only to steal, kill and to destroy.

Yes reader, I eventually repented of my sins and am now trusting God with the rest of my life as his son, Jesus, has taken up residence in my heart. I no longer do the sinful things I used to do.

There at the blessed old Church of God, I met Precious Boyd and made her my beautiful bride. God blessed us with three children we love dearly, our daughter, Tawanna (Tee-Tee), sons, LaMont (Mont) and Michael. His friends call him Mike, but he's Michael to us. I am also thankful for my dear grandchildren, Mekhi (Khi), Malia (Lee-Lee) and Michael, Jr. (MJ). Please forgive all the nicknames.

Bringing it back now to my parents, Vernon and Frances Coleman. They were gifts from God. They were loving, generous, protective, thoughtful Christian parents. They left us for their eternal reward this year, 2020, mere days before their 70th wedding anniversary, passing within 2 days of each other. Their love was endearing and enduring. You will read of them in this book. I miss them more than words can express. They, especially my mother, were the number one fans of my God-inspired poems and often urged that I publish them.

Mom and Dad, in your honor, here it is, "Father…They Know Not What They Do! God's Poetic Reach to a Lost and Dying World." Readers, enjoy and think on the Love of God towards you as you do.

Dedication

I dedicate this book to God, the author and finisher of my faith.

Lord, who shall abide in thy tabernacle? Who shall dwell in thy holy hill?
He that walketh uprightly, and worketh righteousness, and speaketh the truth in his heart.
He that backbiteth not with his tongue, nor doeth evil to his neighbor, nor taketh up a reproach against his neighbor.
Psalm 15:1-3

Special Shout-Outs to:

The Church of God of Chicago-Elder Ricky Dukes, Sr. Pastor. A ministry after God's own heart. The Saints here are loving people and serious about their salvation. Thanks for the love and teaching.

The Church of God-St. Pete, FL. Elder Mary Boyd, Pastor. Seasoned Saints who are soldiers of the cross, knowing no man after the flesh. Thanks for the prayers.

The Church of God-Jackson, MI. Bro. Lee Hampton, Pastor. Preaching and singing under God's inspiration (I view online faithfully). Thanks for the inspiration.

Stephanie A. Wynn Business Solutions
(www.stephanieawynn.com)

Stephanie A. Wynn, Business Development Strategist.

A young lady focused, knowledgeable, innovative, and creative. Thanks for the work.

Profit or Loss

Saints, we truly thank God for the visitors here today, we're thankful they came on-time and without delay. We know there are other places they could have been, but they came here to be with their family or maybe with a friend.

So visitors do enjoy the services and keep an open mind, for the services you will see here will be of a different kind. Many churches just want your money and will give you a show, but the Church of God has a message that you need to know.

Before the message comes forth, I do have a question for you, are you right now ready to meet Jesus if he suddenly breaks the blue? Do you know this day if your soul is showing a profit or a loss? Have you for your soul's sake truly counted the cost?

Dear friend, sin is a loser in this life, there's nothing to be gained, for the wages for sin is death and the devil doesn't want that explained. The gift of God is eternal life to the saved who successfully endure, the people of God have made our calling and election sure.

We have elected to live so that in heaven we can live again, which is why we cried to Jesus to forgive us all our sin. The Bible says, "What shall it profit a man to gain the whole world and lose his own soul?" People do things and they don't know why, it's because sin has taken total control.

The songs we sing here are not just from the lips but also from the heart, did you notice how we started praising God right from the start. We don't play church here because eternity is too long and too serious, we hope that what you hear and see will make you at least curious.

We worship God here in spirit and in truth, the testimonies you hear should give you that proof. Salvation is the only thing that we can enjoy in life and after death, dear visitor, please consider where will you go if today you draw your last breath.

So, we greet you in love and with the utmost respect, all we ask is that today you give your life a "Where will I spend eternity?" check. Check to see if your soul is operating on a profit or a loss, just remember that as the word of God comes across.

The Middleman

The Middleman is very often maligned, his
prices are high and that is by design. He tries
to make a profit no matter the amount, He will
go deep into your pockets on that you can
count.

We shop online but the stores are still a
Middleman, it's best to search for deals
whenever you can. The Middleman will always
think of the bottom line, if he doesn't, he'll be
out of business in just a short time.

The Middleman is someone we usually don't
adore, my thoughts, however, are on a
Middleman who doesn't own a store. This
Middleman never worked a register or put
money in a safe, this Middleman came from far
away, in fact, a heavenly place.

You see, when Adam was created so many
years ago, his heart was pure as heaven, no sin
did Adam know. God gave a wife to Adam to
help him on his way, but in a careless moment
God's word they did disobey.

They knew that God would punish them, they
knew that they had disobeyed, they hid within
the garden, for now, they felt afraid.

When God came there that evening, he drove
them out the gate, he told them of their future
and what would be man's fate.

Everyone born would very soon inherit
terrible, vile sin which truly caused the fall,
and so thus the sin of Adam was passed down
unto us all.

But God so loved the world he soon devised a
plan, to send to us a Godly, Obedient, and
Humble Middle Man.

That Middle Man is Jesus,
God's only Begotten Son,
he stood in the middle between God and man
so our souls could be won. Yes, when the
trumpet sounds and Jesus breaks the blue, tell
me Oh, sinner friend, what do you intend to
do?

When the Book of Life is opened and if Sin is
by your name, are you prepared to suffer in an
endless agonizing Flame? It's time to get
saved from your sins and to stop all the delay,
Satan will soon have your soul if with God you
continue to play.

Nothing or no one on this Earth is worth
going to hell for, so if Jesus is knocking, why
not open Your heart's door.

Jesus had to shed his innocent blood on the
cross, my friends,
He did it so you and I wouldn't be lost in our
sins. He hung on that cross and suffered more
than just a little and just so you know, his
cross was the one in the middle.

The Old Piano

There was an old piano that was dirty and thought to be out of tune, a man decided to auction it off and dragged it into the room. Those in the crowd began to laugh and thought it was a joke, who would bid on that worthless old piano that looks like it's broke?

The crowd said don't auction it off, just go and give it away, no one would want it, not if they know how to play.No one would even consider the old piano, not even giving it a glance,then an old man walked in with a limp and an awkward stance.

The auctioneer saw the man as he gazed at the piano for so very long,then the old man sat down and played a beautiful angelic song. He then cleaned off the old piano and made it look like new, those who didn't glance before now wanted to look and bid on it too.

Dear friends, there was a time our lives were dirty and so out of tune, we were battered and scarred, headed for certain and eternal doom. The devil played us cheap just like that old dirty unwanted piano, knowing if we stayed in sin where Jesus is, we could not even go.

One day, Jesus walked into our lives and cleaned us within, he now abides in our hearts praise God, finally free from sin. The crowd who knew us, saw our lives change but could not understand,now we can say with a smile that this was all part of God's salvation plan.

If there is anyone here today within the sound of my voice and the devil has you bound, then yes today you have a choice. Even as you read this poem, please consider with an open heart, Ask God to help you obtain a much-needed brand new start.

Drexel Boulevard

Welcome guests to the blessed old Church of God in the Windy City on the corner of Drexel Boulevard. It is not your money we desire but give us your ear, because "Thus saith the Lord…" is all you will hear. The teaching and preaching have helped us as we also fervently pray, God's word is molding us so we can stand on that final Judgment Day.

The people we are now, we never used to be, we were people bound by sin, unable to break free. In sin we tried different things to help make us feel better, but it was the devil tricking us because he was far more clever.

We tried drugs or alcohol or fleeting relationships just to have our way, but God kept asking, "How much longer with your soul will you continue to play?" One day we came here many because of being invited, it made the Saints who invited us really very excited.

They knew we would hear something like we had never heard before, We saw genuinely friendly, smiling people soon as we came in the door.

The choir sang so beautifully it made you want to cry, the thought crossed our minds maybe this is the place we want to try.

And then the word came forth in power, in truth, and in spirit, the devil was mad at us because here he never wanted us to visit. As the word came forth, we realized that yes, there is something better, we needed to repent of our sins and accept Jesus as our savior.

So, to the prayer rooms we went, it was time to make things right, we cried out yes to God and boy did that devil take flight. We still come here on Drexel Boulevard so we can grow in God's word, it is our duty to measure up to all the truth that we have heard.

So, plan on giving us a visit here on Drexel Boulevard, visit us in person or online, either way, finding us will not be very hard.

Where Would I Be?

It is time for Tuesday Night Service and where would I be if the Lord should suddenly come? On my knees in prayer? Or out with the crowd just having some fun?

Where would I be? Leading devotion and agreeing in prayer? Or at home drinking tea in my favorite reclining chair?

Where would I be? Getting food for my soul and praying for those that are lost? Or absent again, forgetting the one who bought me at such a great cost?

Where would I be? Raising holy hands and singing songs from the Evening Light Book? Or staying home because too much time at shopping I took?

Where would I be? Listening to testimonies to encourage my soul? Or on my way to join friends for a late-night stroll?

Where would I be? Hearing the ministers preach what thus saith the Lord? Or still taking a nap, not hearing the alarm because of how loud I snored?

Where would I be? Thanking a Saint for fervently praying for me? Or in front of the TV because this Emmy-winning program I just must see?

Where would I be? Rejoicing with the Saints on 46th and Drexel Boulevard? Or pulling up weeds in my well-manicured backyard?

Where would I be? I offered plenty of excusesBut how would they look in his sight? Readers, where do you think I would want Jesus to find me if he should come back on a Tuesday night?

The Day is at Hand

The sins of this world have become a stink in God's nose, soon God will tell Jesus, "Go, get my people. Those whom I've chose". He will tell Gabriel to bring him the Book of Life, the book that contains the names of those who lived right.

The day is at hand when the trumpet shall sound with a noise so loud, the dead will then leave the ground. Christ will appear with Crowns of Victory to give out, only the Saved will get them those who have been devout.

The Saved will arise as Christ and the Angels draw near, the lost and backslidden will try to hide, will try to disappear. The sun and the moon will no longer give light, but the Saints of old, like Moses and Joseph, will be in our sight.

Christ will come for his bride and to judge the world, there will be weeping and wailing, more than any we have heard. Yes, the day to be judged is at hand, coming soon, the Day of the Lord, Saints, to fall off now is something we surely can't afford.

It will be a terrible day, one we must be prepared for, that will be a day that will shake people to their core. Those who played around with God will play with him no more, they haven't got a clue as to the horror they will be in for.

Death angels have been taking to paradise many a faithful Saint, so we must not get weary, we must not faint. The signs of Christ's return seem to be in evidence all around, so Saints, let's be ready, no sin in our lives to be found.

Let us earnestly pray for each other and our unsaved loved ones too, it is time for them to forsake their sin and turn to embrace God's truth. God is reclaiming some while others are being forsaken, their chance to get back to him has been permanently taken.

It's time, Saints, for us to believe that his coming will be here today, that way we'll be ready, ready for Christ to give us our pay. Our pay will be eternal life in that great Heavenly City, to those who won't be ready you truly have my pity.

Saints, let's put a spiritual flashlight on the lives that we lead, let's make sure no spots are there nothing to impede. Saints, the day is at hand, of that we can be sure, let's be certain that we're prepared, let's be sure that we're pure.

Where Will You Spend Eternity?

The trumpet is blowing in Zion let all its inhabitants tremble, for soon the Lord of Hosts and his Angels in the sky will soon assemble. That will be a day there has never been one like, that will be a day of darkness gloominess and fright.

Mighty men, famous men will ask the mountains and rocks for cover, as the Earth begins to melt frantically and in vain they will search to find an altar. Finding no altar, they will try their best to put an end to their life, but death will be no more, no need for guns, no, not even a knife.

Those who played around and put off God one day too many, will see that their condition is permanently stained and filthy. And the Lord shall utter his voice strong and great, for everyone to step into the judgment and learn of their fate.

That day of the Lord will be great and very terrible, he will pronounce judgment on all, clearly and not in parable. Countless regrets will soar high while on their knees sinking low, weeping and gnashing of teeth as their life Jesus begins to show.

"A life free from sin" King Jesus will loudly state, "Is the only life that's going to get thru this heavenly gate." The day that so many people think will never come, will come, it will come with Christ looking for his blood-washed ones.

If there be a sinner within the sound of my voice, consider this an alarm for you this day to make a better choice. If living without Jesus has come to be your plan, then before him at the judgment you won't be able to stand.

Please give thought that all the devil tells you is a lie, he will tell you to put off God until certain things subside. Dear friend we urge you to not put off God any longer, because waiting too long makes your chances for hell-fire stronger.

"Your Angel's Name is Frances."

Once upon a time there was a child ready to be born so one day, he asked God, "They tell me you are sending me down to Earth tomorrow, but how am I going to live there being so small and helpless?"

God replied, "Among the many Angels on earth, I have chosen one for you she will be waiting for you and will take care of you."

The child said, "But here in heaven I don't have to do anything but sing and smile and that is all I need. I am happy here."

God replied, "Your angel will sing for you and will smile at you and will love you. You will be happy there."

The child said, "What if I want to talk to you while I'm down on earth? How will I do it?"

God replied, "your angel will place your hands together and will teach you how to pray."

The child asked, "How will I learn to speak down there?"

God replied, "Your angel, with much patience and care, will teach you how to speak."

The child said, "I have heard there are bad people on earth, who will protect me?"

God replied, "Your angel will always defend you and protect you even if it means risking her own life."

The child said, "But I will always be sad because I will not see you anymore."

God replied, "Your angel will always talk to me about you and she will talk about me to you. She will teach you my word and my way for you to come back to me even though I will always be next to you."

As the child was leaving, he quickly asked God, "Please tell me my angel's name?"

God replied, as he kissed the child farewell on his forehead, "You must hurry now, it is already July 19th on earth. Your angel's name is Frances, You can simply call her Mommy."

(Author's note, July 19 is my birthday. I will never forget the tears my mother shed when I read this to her. I shed tears when I remember that moment. I love and miss her.)

My Wonderful Dad
"Happy Father's Day"

Today I give thanks to my dear Father above, for my wonderful Dad, who has always shown me great love. God richly blessed me with my wonderful Dad. He could have given me any Dad, the choice God made has made me glad.

My wonderful Dad has worked hard all his life, He wants only the best for his children and wife. He works multiple jobs to keep food on the table, It seems like he will work forever as long as he is able.

My wonderful Dad is cautious yet a free hearted soul, He is not going to be fooled and go fall in a financial hole. You won't get him to act until he thinks it through first, he knows that when you're in a hole it is just like you're cursed.

My wonderful Dad is a true family man, he loves for the family to get together whenever it can. He will barbecue some ribs and also some chicken, Ah, the delicious smells he brings to that kitchen.

My Wonderful Dad will drive my mom and brother all over town, he will take them when he gets off work before he even lays down. I wish sometimes that he would get more rest, sometimes he's on the go before his meals can even digest.

My Wonderful Dad is a man I greatly admire, he's a man that's been tested and came through the fire. My Wonderful Dad is a living legacy, I hope he stays healthy and lives longer than me.

VERNON & FRANCES

SEPTEMBER 10,1950

Is when they said, "I do",they exchanged their vows promising to stay true. Only a few people were there including her mom & dad, their wedding made the other men who wanted her very, very sad.

Vernon & Frances now embarked on a whole new life; she would try her very best to be a good housewife. He would work so hard to try to make ends meet, soon after came the pitter patter of June's little feet.

Times were hard as their little family started to grow, it was just a couple of years later when little June got a little bro'. Vernon & Frances looked to God to help them make it through, they now had another mouth to feed, I made little mouth number two.

Divorces were increasing throughout the United States, Vernon & Frances though were still true soul mates. Once close families were now being torn apart, not Vernon & Frances, their love was embedded deep in their hearts.

Their marriage was not always peaches and cream, it was then that on their love and on their Lord, they would more firmly lean. Sometimes the devil would put their marriage under attack, Vernon & Frances refused to put their hand to the plough and then turn back.

They bought a beautiful home on 64th & Langley, it was here that Van was born and welcomed to the family. Frances' parents and good schools were just a short distance away, and June & I now had good friends with whom we could play.

Their love was never broken, only Frances bones seemed to do that, I'm glad she never tripped over Puff, our dear beloved cat. Vernon loved to talk about sports, baseball he loved the best, oh how he hated it when the Cubs lost to the '69 Mets.

Their love just grew as all the years flew by. Their love was still strong when we thought that Vernon would die. He was struck by a bullet that wasn't meant for him, our life at 64th & Langley suddenly got very, very dim.

Frances stayed at the hospital, rarely leaving his side, she showed love and courage because she was still his bride. God looked down from above on Vernon's devoted wife, because of her love and prayers, God extended his life.

The years have flew by, the children are all grown, June has, and I have grown children of our own. The grandkids and great-grandkids love their "Nana" and "Bay-Bay". We all love them on this their 59th anniversary day.

So there, I've told the story of my beloved Mom and Dad, to be the son of Vernon & Frances, I couldn't be more glad. On September 10, 1950, Vernon & Frances made a pact, today, 59 years later, thanks be unto God, their marriage is still intact.

Now we can hardly wait to give them a good cheer, a cheer that will ring out this exact time next year. A cheer that will be so very loud and hearty, good Lord willing at Vernon & Frances 60th wedding anniversary party.

9/10/2009

When God is Calling

God's Saints will be glad to see the Lord and his heavenly host breaking the blue, Those who rejected him will be weeping as Jesus says, "It's time I judge you!" Saints, let us hold fast, in our salvation we truly must prevail, the devil will want us to lose out, to let our experience with God get stale.

Beloved, it is not because God is not talking that people do not hear, the Bible says, dear friend, that it is only because people have stopped-up their ears.

To dwell with Christ above we must live for him here below, if death or the trumpet catches us in sin, then with Christ above we cannot go.

Did you know that millions of souls are drifting down to hell? Including, many who from their salvation fell, backsliders, be reconciled to God before your destiny he seals, because then Christ will be your judge and not your court of appeals.

Yes, the act of a choice can fix our eternal fate, beloved, will it be the Lake of Fire or heaven's pearly gate?

Today may be the day that God will call you just once more, upon that call, say yes to him and let Jesus in your heart's door.

Take the Utmost Precaution

Praise God, he delivered us from a world of sin and shame, all praises to him that in the Book of Life, he wrote our name. No longer are we cast down and bound forever in sin, Thanks be unto Jesus for being our savior and our very best friend.

We're now new creatures loving it when service nights come around, you know the Saints will all be singing and making a joyful sound. The devotional leaders are always a little nervous, but we give that no bother, we all join in prayer asking God to fill our service with power.

The word of God is preached, and boy, we eat it up, the messages are always stirring and truly fill our cup. After services, Saints like to talk, laugh and encourage one another, We want no one going out and making a spiritual blunder.

However, Satan got angry, saying it is too many in God's church hearing God's word, He told his imps it's time for us to go in there and thin their herd.

Satan said evening services there have too many worshipping in those pews, let's get some of them to put those evenings to a different kind of use.

So, Saints, let us be careful not to make evening services an option. When it comes to our souls, we must take the utmost precautions. Yes, we always want to live a life free from sin, but don't forget that a seat in heaven is something we must win.

You know the story, the ten virgins with the lamps, they were all without sin. But five of them to the wedding didn't make it in. They gave no attention that their oil was no more, Saints, being all we can be for God is something we can't ignore.

Yes, things can come up and make us miss service here or there, just let the Saints know how you're doing so we can keep you in prayer. But to those who can come out but simply choose not to, like the virgins that made it in, we don't have enough oil for you.

Facing the Judgment

Facing means going towards or coming near, please give me your attention with a heart that can hear. The times we are living in is drawing Judgment so nigh, yes, dear friends, Jesus will soon break the sky.

Did you know Sodom & Gomorrah was not as bad as today? People are no longer seeking God but trusting in their own way. Abraham tried to intervene for those cities but couldn't find many just, God can't continue to look upon sin, to him destroying it is a must.

Only God's mercy has spared us Sodom & Gomorrah's fate, it is time to turn back to God before the everlasting too late. Families are killing their own with little thought and no remorse, dear friends, God will not allow us to stay on that sinful course.

Yes, it is true no man knows the day or even the hour, the day that Jesus returns full of majesty and great power. God has given us the signs, he left them in his Word, unfortunately, man has strayed so far God's instruction is no longer heard.

This country once embraced God's teaching and his laws, our country has turned its back, now laden with sinful flaws. The USA doesn't even want God's name spoken in schools, our courts won't even allow it, they're just a court of fools.

Every minute that ticks by brings us closer to that day, the day that many will try to hide, and many will try to pray. There will be no time to pray, They'll be no place to hide, Heaven will greet only those that in him continued to abide.

The time is now to reflect and to truly count the cost, is there anything on this earth worth my soul being lost? When Jesus breaks the sky and eternity begins, how tragic it would be if you're still holding onto your sins.

People say that when that day comes, God's too good to let anyone suffer, but that will only apply to those who used Jesus as a buffer. Yes, eternal suffering awaits those who would not his Son accept. Oh, how Satan tricked them into the worse kind of Neglect.

He that hath an ear, please do give heed, It is time to put away foolish things and any dirty deed. It is time to get ready for the next life to come, It is time to live for Christ, God's only begotten son.

We go to bed at night hoping to face another day, how do we know that will or won't be when Jesus is on his way? Do you want to gamble with your soul as though it were dice? That could be the day we all enter into eternal life.

Where do you want to spend your eternity? I choose Heaven with all its peace and serenity. Too many will choose Hell because these words they won't believe. Making them think there's plenty of time is how Satan will deceive.

Be watchful, be vigilant, be ready is my rallying cry, do not be caught in your sins on the day that time will die. He gave us the signs, in the book many a hint, yes, dear ones, we are facing the Judgment.

The Church of God

Everyone seems to agree that time is going so fast, it just seems that this world too much longer, won't be able to last. Too many people are ignoring God's signs of the end, the world is now saturated with a sin and hypocrisy blend.

Saints, it's a blessing to be saved at such a time as this, a time when so many seem to feel that ignorance is bliss. Many do not even want to hear anything spoken about God's word so true, too many today think that the golden rule is, "Just do You"

Brand new mega-churches seem to be popping up all over the land, their pastors telling people it is better to worship God in buildings so grand. It's these pastors that are being worshipped, draining people's money as they pretend to be God's servants.

Let's think back to Jacob when he dreamed of a ladder in the sky, Angels pure he saw upon it, and yes, God was standing nigh.

When the morning came in splendor, and from dreaming he awoke, he was frightened for a moment for he knew that God had spoke.

'Twas the gateway into heaven, Jacob announced so sure, and sometime in the future God will have a church so pure. And the pillow which Jacob slept on, which was only a stone, was soon set up as a pillar for a House where God is known.

Yes, that house of God is the almighty Church of God, a place where the saved and sanctified in holiness do trod. Jacob said it was a dreadful place, the same holds true today, it's a place where you can only be a member if Christ took your sins away.

It is divinely ruled, no set program is given to follow, here the word is given, that in sin, no one has to wallow. The Church of God is certainly like no other, she is the only church borne of her mother.

My friends, other churches will tell you to do the best you can, they don't tell you that if you do, it is in hell you surely will land.

If the only requirement for heaven is "Just do the best, you can", then what was the need of Christ to suffer and die at the hands of sinful man?

I am glad the Church of God is truly like no other, there is no phoniness in her, not in one saved sister, not in one saved brother. O Church of God, I love thy courts, thou mother of the free, thou blessed home of all the saved, I dwell content in thee.

God's Church & the Virus

Life as we know it has taken on a change, much of what we love to do, we've had to rearrange. A virus pandemic has appeared and spread world-wide, many people have contracted the virus and many people have died.

The Saints of God have been affected as well for many of us it has changed the way we dwell, staying at home was once a choice but now a must. Not just for the sick and elderly but also for those young and robust.

Social distancing is now a government decree, it is one of the ways to stop the virus most do agree. Most people have chosen to panic and to live in fear, they are putting their trust in doctors to make it disappear.

The Saints of God cannot assemble as we love to do, because the virus became more deadly and treacherously grew The Pastor and ministers, our watchmen on the wall, they knew they would have to make an unprecedented call.

The call was to suspend church service, hoping not to get anyone sick, remember though, God's church is not made up of mortar or of brick. God's church is his people united in love, gratitude, trust, and praise, people who are no longer burdened by sin, deceit and devilish ways.

God has not given us the spirit of fear, God has made that crystal clear. He has given us power, love and a sound mind, He has given us the courage to face these uncertain times.

Saints, let's draw closer to God, while we're away from each other, let's call, let's fast and let us pray for one another. God has a plan with this virus, on that you can be sure, so during His plan, let's make sure that we stay pure.

We will assemble again together, Saints, one day soon, let's continue to be safe, to the virus we are not immune. Let's stay saved because our next meeting could be in the sky, where we can give this virus and the devil a final good-bye.

He Still Went Up That Hill

Once a long time ago, God made some things, he made the Heavens and the Earth where the birds do sing. In 6 days, he made everything that he wanted to make, God saved the best for last, making Adam and his mate.

Nothing came between Adam and his Father, Adam was beloved and a very good gardener. We all know however that the bliss didn't last very long, for soon, Adam and his mate did something very wrong.

Their act of disobedience separated man from God, man's relationship with God was now tainted and flawed. The devil was now revealed as man's true enemy, sin and man were now bound together for eternity.

Adam & Eve had children and now sin began to spread, mankind was now without hope, the outlook full of dread.

The atonement for sin was animal sacrifices which God grew tired of, God wanted a better sacrifice but that could only come from above.

God's beloved son, Jesus, was the only one worthy of such a sacrifice, Jesus told his father, "Wrap me in flesh and I'll go give my life." Jesus came to earth but to sin he would not yield, the very nation Jesus came to save only wanted him killed.

God decided that Jesus' sacrifice would be for all men, Jew or Gentile, just had to repent and turn away from sin. Jesus in Gethsemane wrestled with what he had to do, he knew he had to die on a hill, die for me and die for you.

Jesus knew that his blood they would soon spill, Jesus, though, he still went up that hill. Jesus knew dying on the cross would give his accusers a thrill, Saints and friends, Jesus still went up that hill.

The payment had to be made for our adultery, fornication, lies and cheating, to pay our sin debt, Jesus was whipped and took a harsh beating. Jesus suffered for us only wanting to do God's will, despite all that suffering, he still went up that hill.

Up on that hill, an old, rugged cross was awaiting, watching Jesus draw his last breath, the soldiers were anticipating. There were two men hanging there already and one chose to vent, the other thief looked upon Jesus and from his heart did repent.

My sins and your sins were there right beside those rusty nails, some with sins so horrible you would never give the details.

Those sins were not his, we should have been given the bill, but God so loved the world he sent his only son up that hill.

I love Jesus for dying in my place, I live for him now, justified by his grace. If you're lost in sin, cry out to God in sorrow as you kneel, because, yes, for you, he still went up that hill.

Listen To The Testimonies

Saints, don't you agree that life is better without sin in it? We seem to appreciate more each God-given day, we must admit. God has brought us to a new family of love and support, A new family that fears God and is of a good report.

Saints, Thank God, he has cast our sins so very far away, that it can't even be found with the GPS's of today. I dare you to try to Google Map where your sins are; there's no way they can be found, not even with modern radar.

But Saints, sometimes the devil will tell us that we're all alone; that all our tests and trials are because of what we have sown. Satan will tell us no one else is going through that test; he'll say, "Don't call on Jesus, just try to do your best."

Saints, let's keenly listen to the testimonies that are given; because then we can see that some tests are truly quite common. Some other Saints have unsaved loved ones that burden their heart; some other Saints have a family the devil is trying to tear apart.

Some other Saints have found themselves deep in financial straits; some other Saints have various pains and aches. Some other Saints have children that won't obey and misbehave; Some other Saints have just buried loved ones in the cemetery grave.

So, Saints, yes, our tests sometimes hurt and make us cry, it is then that Satan will hope that we kiss our salvation goodbye. But Saints, the tests coming against us are just for a season, to not go through the test, well, there is no good reason.

So, in my tests, I'm trusting in God and leaning on you; so far that formula has been carrying me through. So, when those tests come that drives me to my knees; what am I doing? I'm listening to your testimonies.

The Blessed Day

Saints, before we were born, God knew us; But would we prove to be unjust or just? We were all born in sin, Satan, our evil boss, he kept us in sin so our one soul would be lost.

Then one day, we knew there had to be more to life, how hard it was to constantly be in toil, to constantly be in strife. We thought that church-going might make life more sweet, we tried that and found we still weren't complete.

We saw that church folk often drank the hardest, we saw that church folk often cursed the loudest. We saw that church folk often gossiped against their neighbor, we saw that church folk often, like us, in sin did labor.

We shunned the church world and just stayed in sin; then, one day, there was a knock on the door from a dear, dear friend.

He said come to me if you're burdened and want a better way; I will dwell in your heart and take you out of that sinful miry clay.

Sin was all we knew with all its death and doubt; but Jesus said, "Forgiving your sin is what I'm all about." Crushed by the weight, we fell on bended knee; Jesus said, "Come taste of me and liberty you will see."

We tried this, and we tried that, and nothing could satisfy; so, we cried out to God, "Save me! Your salvation I will try." Thank God how he cleaned us, our journey set for Glory, we're so glad to be in the Church of God to hear the Gospel story.

So, join me, Saints, and let's give God all hispraise, for being under ministers that fear God and to him always prays. Saints, let's tell the world that Satan is a lie! Saint's, let's always show Christ until the blessed day we die. Amen.

One Door Leads to Another

Please incline your ear to me, my dear sister and brother; were you aware that in this life we lead, one door leads to another. Christ said, "I am the door, by me, you enter in." But you won't make heaven if you still abide in sin.

How many doors did Satan spread the welcome mat for us? We naively entered those doors into evil and worldly lust. He knew if he kept us in, that one door to another it would lead; he knew the door of hell was connected to the sins we didn't flee.

Sometimes we tried on our own to leave back out a certain door, Satan said, "Wait, it's going to get better, what are you leaving for?" He quickly ushered us into another door with different sights and sounds, the door was different however, sin there did still abound.

Our misery grew more and the doorknob always seemed out of reach; we saw people doing all types of sin, some who on Sundays would get up to preach.

47

Christ one day beckoned and said, "I have opened the door." "Come unto me if you are heavy laden and you need not sin anymore." We said, "Lord, is it thru another door that we have to trod?" He said, "Yes, I am that Door if you want to get to God."

So, we went thru the Door so we could live to live again; we are so glad he opened the Door and forgave us of all our sin. Saints, let's stay hid in Christ, so he leads us to that final door, the Door that leads to peace on that distant heavenly shore. Amen.

Vernon & Frances, Part II

September 10, 1950, is when they said, "I do" They exchanged vows promising to stay true. Only a few people were there including her Mom and Dad, their wedding made the other men who wanted her very, very sad.

Vernon and Frances now embarked on a whole new life, she would try her best to be a good housewife. He would work so hard to make ends meet, soon after came the pitter-patter of June's little feet.

Times were hard as their little family grew, it was just a couple of years later when little June got a little Bro'. Vernon and Frances looked to God to help them make it through, they now had another mouth to feed, I made little mouth number two.

Divorces were increasing throughout the United States, Vernon and Frances, though, were still true soul mates. Once close families were now being torn apart, Not Vernon and Frances, their love was embedded deep in their hearts.

Their marriage was not always, peaches and cream, Then on their love and on their Lord they would more firmly lean. Sometimes the devil would put their marriage under attack, Vernon and Frances refused to put their hand to the plough and then turn back.

They bought a beautiful home on 64th and Langley, here Van was born and welcomed to the family. Frances' parents and good schools were just a short distance away, June and I now had good friends with whom we could play.

My parent's love was never broken, only Frances' bones seemed to do that, I am glad she never tripped over Puff, who was our dear beloved cat. Vernon loved to talk about sports, baseball he loved the best, oh, how he hated it when the Cubs lost to the '69 Mets.

They knew that it wasn't always going to be sunshine and blue skies, but what God puts together can't be broken no matter how hard Satan tries.

Van, June, and I owe them such a huge debt of thanks, over the years we have begged and borrowed more money than in some banks. But money was not the most valuable thing they gave us, they gave us love, they taught us to be responsible and they showed us how to trust.

They gave more to us when it meant having less for them, they taught us how to call on the Lord and make him our friend. They never blamed each other when things didn't go right, they rebuked the devil when he said, "From this marriage, go, take flight."

Their love just grew as the years flew by, their love was still strong when we thought that Vernon would die. He was struck by a bullet not meant for him, our life at 64th and Langley suddenly got very, very dim.

Frances stayed at the hospital, rarely leaving his side, she showed love and courage because she was still his bride. God looked down from above on Vernon's devoted wife, because of her love and prayers, God extended his life.

The years have flown by, the children are all grown, June has, and I have grown children of our own. The grandkids and great-grandkids love their "Grandma Sweet and Bay-Bay" We all love them on this their 60th Anniversary Day.

I thank God for this day, in all his wondrous glory, that we are all here to celebrate this amazing, true love story. For you see, Vernon and Frances set the marriage bar high, but I pledge to them and to my wife that to reach for it, I will always try.

So, there, I have told the story of my beloved Mom and Dad, to be the son of Vernon and Frances, I couldn't be more glad. On September 10, 1950, Vernon and Frances made a pact, today, 60 years later, thanks be unto God, their marriage is still intact.

(Written under God's inspiration on 09/10/10, on their 60th Wedding Anniversary.)

Satan Wants Us Back

Oh, Saints, remember how the devil did us so wrong? But God saved us and put in our hearts a brand-new song. We ran for our lives fearing to look back, we made sure our prayer lives were tight, not allowing any slack.

We passed out tracts, no services would find us absent, our praise to the Lord was never less than constant. God's word was always a joy for us to hear; our love of God was only surpassed by our fear.

While once we were members of Satan's doomed ranks; we praise God now to be free, to him, we owe thanks. Yes, Saints, we went from doomed to miraculously delivered, thank God, Satan's plan for us divinely got altered.

But Saints, ever wonder why Satan presses us sore? It's because in hell, he knows there's room for one more.

He wants us back, so he mocks us when we are tried, he tells us we're not saved, no longer Christ's dear bride.

He tells us it doesn't take all that, ease up a little bit, but he knows if we ease up, soon after we will quit. He tries to tell us, "Come back, you're missing all the fun." But looking back is what Lot's wife never should have done.

Saints, let's encourage and pray earnestly for each other; remember Jesus, our Savior, is our precious soul's anchor. Let's follow the Church of God teaching down to the letter; it's only going to help our experience with God get that much better.

So, Saints, pray for this poet as I expose that devil; No Satan! We refuse to go back and stoop to your level. Pastor Gordon, Pastor Hampton, and other Saints of old; are pulling for us because eternity is right on the threshold.

So yes, Saints, the devil has put a target on our backs; but the Blood of the Lamb protects us from his attacks. Remember, no weapon formed against us shall prosper; so, let's stay under the blood, my sister, my brother.

Christ Was The Highest Bidder

Saints, remember how we were so lost in sin; looking for a way out only to be deceived again. Didn't we get so tired of being sick and tired, We got tired of being used, cheated, shamed, and fired.

We wandered, smoked, lied, lusted, drank and drugged; it's like we had holes in our life that was never plugged. We knew we needed something but searched all the wrong places; new things we sought out only brought new curses.

Some of us perhaps thought that we were not that bad but, remarkably, we could never figure out why we often stayed so sad. We decided it was time that life showed us a better way; but all life showed us one day to the next was another replay.

One day, Saints, we realized that our souls were on the auction block; while still bound by Satan, one day on our heart was a knock.

Jesus said, "Dear loved one, won't you let me in, I'll be your shepherd and forgive all your sin."

Satan said, "Don't listen to him, you know I'm your friend" So we stayed with Satan and all the replays started all over again. We said that's enough, this is an auction, let the bidding begin, whoever bids the highest, our soul gets to win.

Satan offered cars, money, fame and all the fun we could handle, he said, 'I'll make sure you are loved and never involved in a scandal." Then Jesus spoke to us and oh, how our hearts did burn; he said, "I will give you the peace and joy of which your soul does yearn.

So, Satan bid worldly goods for our "soul to keep" top bid, but all he offered was the woeful things we already did. We cried, "Jesus, can you beat Satan's offer of the same old mud; Jesus said, "Dear one, for my top bid, I offered my blood."

Jesus said, "My blood that was spilled on Calvary's Cross; is the same blood that will keep your soul from being lost.

My blood, no man took it from me, for it I freely gave, whoever is covered by my blood never has to fear the grave."

Thank God, the auction over, Christ was the highest bidder; our souls have been rescued, now no longer a sinner. Saints, let's always give thanks to the Lord and let our light so shine, because the blood on that cross should have been yours andit should have been mine.

Adam & Eve & You

There are two Bible characters almost everyone knows, they lived blissfully in a garden until trouble arose, the two Bible characters you already know I believe, of course, those two characters are Adam and Eve.

They lived in bliss with not a care to their name, they wore no clothes but there was no need for shame. They talked with God, maybe even every day, I am sure in that garden they thought they would always stay.

God forbade them nothing except for one tree to leave alone, there was fruit on that tree that God himself had grown. There was no shortage of fruit, it was everywhere to be found, there was luscious fruit and tasty fruit Adam grew from the ground.

Peace and harmony prevailed so Satan decided to interfere, Satan used a subtle serpent whose motives to Eve were unclear. Satan knew that he had only to get Eve to lend an ear, soon peace and harmony began to disappear.

Eve disobeyed God by eating from the one tree that God said do not eat, instead of feeling shame, she turned and gave it to Adam as though it were a treat. Soon God came walking in the cool of the day, "Adam, where art thou?" they heard God say.

Instead of running towards God, they chose to run and hide, they soon realized that the subtle serpent to them had lied. Their disobedience was a clear act of sin, mankind's sorrows were just about to begin.

Centuries later, Satan is still deceiving folks, do not be one who blindly falls for his hoax. Do not do as Adam and Eve and turn your back on God, shame and fear would engulf you wherever you looked to trod.

Death could catch you as you recklessly go about, or Jesus and his angels could come back with such a triumphant shout. If God is not talking to you then you should have great concern, because if things go unchanged, in hell you will certainly burn.

A burden of sin and fear could be more than you could bare, maybe you're putting up a front on the outside, inside a soul in despair. If you are a prodigal son or daughter, don't you want to come home? Nevermore to stray from God. Nevermore to roam.

Don't listen to those false preachers that say, "Do the best you can." In hell, it will be burning hot flames that those preachers will try to fan. Give your life to Jesus. Accept him as your savior in this pandemic year, sincerely ask for forgiveness of your sins before Jesus should reappear.

Get down on bended knee and to God, pray through, do not let a sad story be written of Adam and Eve and You.

Robert

I remember all the good times we shared, family, love, and understanding was always there. I remember how you walked us all to school, making sure we were there on time to learn the "Golden Rule".

I will miss your voice so baritone, so beautiful and grand, I remember how it seemed like you could fix anything by hand. I remember how you made us clean when Mom and Dad was at work, you made us scrub those walls until all our fingers hurt.

When we talked, you listened intently and always gave good advice, I always took your advice to heart never did you have to tell me twice. Through your illness, you were brave and trusted God to help you endure, I know you are with him now because through it all with God, you made your calling and election sure.

Robert, I will miss you dearly, you have always been in my life. Without you now, life somehow will not seem right. Robert, I am glad you are not suffering in pain anymore, I know for sure you are walking around now on heaven's golden floor.

(Author's note: Co-authored with my wife, Precious, as she described life with her brother, Robert Boyd.)

The Stanton Letter

December 16, 2009

Dear Mr. & Mrs. Stanton,

Please forgive me for this intrusion into your day. This letter has hopefully been forwarded to you. My name is Vernon L. Coleman. I have never met you or any member of your family. But I was touched and moved by the article I read in the newspaper regarding the life and death of your beloved son.

I, myself, have a 4 year-old grandson whom I love dearly and it would be devastating to lose him, especially at that age. Therefore, I am very sorry that you have to be in such immense pain.

Please take comfort, if you can, in knowing and being assured that your son is now in heaven. Mr. Stanton, that same hug your son gave you; he is now giving to Jesus and Jesus is returning the same hug you gave. There is much joy there and good fun. Your son was chosen to be a play leader and that infectious smile of his will never leave his face throughout eternity.

Don't forget that in Mark 10:14, Jesus said, "Suffer the little children to come unto me, and forbid them not: for of such is the Kingdom of God." Mr. & Mrs. Stanton, please do not begrudge Jesus for taking your son, suffer him, which means let him go to Jesus. Rejoice in the everlasting life that your son now has.

Your son has simply changed addresses. His former home was with you. His present and forever address is in heaven. Jesus gave you stewardship over him for 4 years and from what I read in the paper, Mr. & Mrs. Stanton, your stewardship was filled with love and attention towards him. Be proud that in his short time on Earth, he gave much of that love and attention he received from you to others who needed it. You will be rewarded for that.

I have taken enough of your time. I just wanted to extend to you, words of comfort and solace and pray for you and your family ever since I read the article. Please know that your son is waiting on you guys to join him while he hugs Jesus and plays with the angels. To him, it won't be a long time, because time doesn't exist in heaven. It only exists here on Earth. II Peter 3:8 says, "But, beloved, be not ignorant of this one thing, that one day is with the Lord as a thousand years, and a thousand years as one day." So, no matter how long you live, when you join him, it will seem to him like you came just a little later.

Just continue to spread the love, attention, and joy that your son did and others will see him in your lives, which will keep him alive on Earth while he lives in heaven. God bless you and my prayers will continue for you as you grieve.

Hanna

You wanted to simply get out of the rain, when a cowardly triggerman decided to cause someone pain. He hopped over a fence and started shooting at others, too cowardly to fight, he sprayed out a death sentence, then cowardly took flight.

You were struck, your face, lovely enough to take away one's breath, your face now represents youngsters who have met violent, premature death. How does one come to admire a girl he never knew, the triggerman took such a beautiful star, of that, he had no clue.

Everyone talks of your grace, your charm, your beauty, and your smile, for someone so young, it seems you had an energetic, engaging style.

You twirled, you danced, you laughed, and you stood out in a crowd, you aced all of your classes making your family so very proud.

I hope that your tragic death did not come in vain, I hope it makes gangbangers   realize violence offers nothing to gain.

Do they comprehend that the violence they embrace will one day visit them, their prospects for longevity seems to daily grow more dim.

The time has come for them all to lay their shiny guns down, Spring is coming and we need flowers and more Hannas to abound.

Farewell Mrs. Rodgers

It is time to celebrate and applaud all that you have done, Mrs. Rodgers, our respect, love, and admiration you've won. The time has come that you have chosen to step aside, you deserve to sit back and just let life simply glide.

Your dedication and leadership have been second to none, take pride in your accomplishments and the work you have done. Our school has been a better school while under your guidance, We will always appreciate your thoughtfulness, inspiration, and kindness.

You gave the school, your all, with even your family pitching in, you put in such long hours as though some days would never end. Now no more punching the clock or deadlines to meet, no more walking the halls to make sure the students are in their seats.

We will remember the wonderful parties you gave to your staff, it was good to see you relax and get a much-needed chance to laugh. Now it is our turn, Mrs. Rodgers, to throw you a party that's swell, here's prayerfully wishing you God's blessings as we sadly bid you farewell.

(Author's note: Co-authored with my wife, Precious, as she described working with her former Principal.)

God is Able!

I wonder, have you ever heard two people having an argument and one says to the other, "You better check yourself!" In that context, it is meant as a statement of contention or anger or warning. Today, brothers and sisters, I'm not mad or angry with you, however, I'm here to let you know that you need to check yourself. Check yourself to see if you're being all and everything God wants you to be.

He wants you and me to be overcomers. He wants us to overcome the things that Satan throws against us. He wants us to overcome because he enables us to be overcomers every day of our lives.

Check yourself to see if you are an overcomer or not. Hebrews 3:8 tells us that God has put all things in subjection under our feet. It tells us that God left nothing that is not put under our feet. We are to walk on, step on, trample on, or even stomp on anything under our feet.

God wants us to put our problems and temptations under our feet, not the other way around. They should not be tap-dancing on our head. They should be under our feet. God wants us to meet our problems head-on. God does not want us to run from our problems or go around them, he wants us to defeat our problems through him so he will be glorified. God wants to partner with us in our problems. He gives us the grace to go through the problems. We give him the glory he deserves for the victory.

In Exodus 6:29 & 30, God tells Moses to speak unto Pharaoh, king of Egypt and tell him all that God has to say. But Moses asks God how is it that Pharaoh is going to listen to him? God tells Moses in this chapter, he has made Moses a god to Pharaoh. God was telling Moses, Pharaoh ain't got nothing on you Moses because I, God, the Great I Am, the beginning and the end, the Master of the Universe, the Creator of all creation, the All-Knowing, have made you a god to Pharaoh.

Brothers and Sisters, if you believe, if you accept that God is an able God, if you love him and cherish and keep his word, then he will make you and me a god to whatever comes against us.

Face your fears and problems head on just as Moses did with Pharaoh. Moses took on Pharaoh face to face, not giving an unqualified opinion but telling him what thus saith the Lord.

Moses gave Pharaoh God's word. We need God's word to face our Pharaohs. It is good to hear what the preacher is saying but sometimes you have got to get God's word one on one just like Moses did. Moses was alone and in the backside of the desert when he heard from God.

We have to get alone sometimes so we can hear what God will tell us regarding our problems. Sometimes the preacher won't have the word for you, but God does, always has, always will.

John 1:1 states that "In the beginning was the Word, and the Word was with God, and the Word was God." If God was able to part the Red Sea so his people could walk on dry ground, he is still able enough to help you pay your bills and get financially on solid ground. If God was able enough to bring down the walls of Jericho, he is still able enough to bring down discord in your home and make your spouse and children act right.

If God was able enough to kill an 11-foot giant named Goliath with a single rock, he is still able enough to help you find a job with a single resume. If God was able enough to move Elijah from earth to heaven on a chariot of fire, he is still able enough to move you to a better neighborhood. If God was able to heal back in the day, then he is still able to heal in our day.

How do I know that? Because my Bible, in Hebrews, Chapter 13, tells me that he is the same yesterday, today, and forever and the fact that he has been a miracle worker in my life.

He is able to give, are you able to receive? He is able to bless, are you able to believe. He is able to be victorious, are you able to fight? He is able to save, are you able to accept? God is able!

Will You Choose Wisely?

Beloved, we all love to be entertained one way or another. Some like to be entertained with good music. Some like to be entertained with a good play. Some like to be entertained with comedy, while some like to be entertained with a good movie. An entertaining movie came out in 1989, entitled "Indiana Jones and the Last Crusade." Perhaps, some of you saw it. Indiana Jones was an adventurous archeologist always looking for lost treasures.

In this movie, Indiana Jones was searching for the cup that Jesus drank from at the Last Supper. The cup is often called the Holy Grail. I will not try to tell you about the whole movie, but there is a part I do want to mention.

In the movie, Indiana Jones was searching for the Holy Grail, but so were the German Nazis under orders from Hitler. The Nazis, who represented evil, hired their own archeologist to find the Grail before Jones could and they tried to hinder Jones in his search. Jones found the cave where the Grail was but unknown to him, the Nazis followed him. Jones and the Nazi archeologist found a Medieval Knight guarding a table which had many cups on

74

it. The Knight would not tell either of them which one was the Holy Grail, he told them they would have to choose for themselves. However, beloved, he also told them, "Choose wisely, for while the true Grail will bring you life, the false Grail will take it from you."

The Nazi pushed Jones aside to select the Grail for himself. He saw a cup laden with rubies and diamonds and felt the cup was worthy of a king. He took the cup and dipped it in water and drank from it. He withered up and died. The Knight responded, "He chose poorly." Jones then selected a cup that looked ordinary and common. He dipped it in water and drank from it. He did not die. The Knight responded, "You have chosen wisely."

Brothers and sisters, my topic today is "Will You Choose Wisely?"

When God created Adam and Eve, he gave them a beautiful garden to live in and care for. He gave them dominion over all the animals. He also gave them a unique gift he, to this day, gives us. He gave them the gift of free will. God had given them instruction to not eat of the tree of the knowledge of good and evil, but he gave them the free will whether to obey or disobey that instruction. They had a choice. Unfortunately, for them and all of mankind, they chose poorly.

Beloved, before I go too deep into my topic, I want to break down for you that scenario in the Garden of Eden when they chose poorly. In I John 2:16-17, the Bible says, "For all that is in the world, the lust of the flesh, and the lust of the eyes, and the pride of life, is not of the father, but is of the world. And the world passeth away, and the lust thereof: but he that doeth the will of God abideth forever."

When Adam and Eve ate of that tree, they chose not to do the will of God. In the Bible, Genesis 3:6 tells us that, "When the woman saw that the tree was good for food, and that it was pleasant to the eyes, and a tree to be desired to make one wise, she took of the fruit thereof, and did eat, and gave also unto her husband with her; and he did eat."

Let's break that down, the scripture said in part, "When the woman saw that the tree was good for food..." Beloved, she chose not to do the will of God but to satisfy the lust of the flesh.

She wasn't hungry, they had plenty to eat. Eve wanted to taste what they were forbidden to have. She wanted to satisfy that lust of the flesh. You know there are things God may give you and not give me because maybe my flesh won't act right if I have it, and the same goes for you. The scripture also says in part, "...and that it was pleasant to the eyes..." Beloved, she chose not to do the will of God but to satisfy the lust of the eyes. God had given them many beautiful trees and plants to look upon. Eve looked upon the wrong thing. You know, sometimes we need to be mindful of what we look at. We need to look harder at what God has given us and not what the devil is showing us.

The scripture says in part, "and a tree to be desired to make one wise..." Beloved, she was more concerned with the pride of life, she wanted to elevate her station in life, she wanted to be as a god rather than obeying God. Proverbs 16:18 tells us that, "Pride goeth before destruction, and an haughty spirit before a fall."

Beloved, be thankful for the blessings God has given us, but don't let those things fill you up with pride and leave you with a haughty spirit instead of a humble spirit.

If you're full of pride and don't have the right spirit, expect a fall.

Speaking of a fall, thanks to Adam and Eve, mankind was marked for destruction and damnation. We fell from the Grace of God. But thanks be to God, he gave us another gift. You see, we were in deep trouble because Adam and Eve mishandled God's gift of free will. God knew that they could show no greater love to him than by freely obeying his word, by obeying not because they had to but because they wanted to.

As parents, aren't we proudest of our children when they obey our instructions even when we aren't around? We're not physically with them but lovingly, they obey our instruction as though we were. How disappointed God was in Adam and Eve.

Had Adam and Eve handled God's gift properly, had they chosen wisely, they would have lived forever in that garden in peace and joy. If someone buys you a beautiful sweater as a gift and you go out and wash your car with it, you have mishandled the gift. You have used the gift in an unappreciative manner. Yes, your car is now clean, but the intent of the gift is unfulfilled.

God gave us another gift, his only begotten son, Jesus. We can accept him as our savior and trade our life for his or we can reject the trade, reject his son and live life as we see fit. We can choose to satisfy the lust of the flesh, the lust of the eye and the pride of life as Adam and Eve did. But please remember what the old medieval knight said in the movie, "Choose wisely, for while the true Grail will bring you life, the false Grail will take it from you." Remember, Jesus is the cup of life, the true Holy Grail. The Book of Psalms tells us to taste and see that the Lord is good and blessed is the man that trusts in him.

The Book of Acts lets us know that Stephen trusted in God. In the 7th chapter of Acts and the 8th verse the Bible says that Stephen was full of faith and power and did great wonders and miracles among the people. There is a word in the dictionary I want to define for you. The word is "Incongruent" Webster's defines it as lacking harmony or agreement of parts, unsuitable, inappropriate. Note that the Bible said Stephen was full of faith and power. If you are calling yourself a Christian or a child of God or a follower of Jesus and you don't have faith to believe God and the power to live right, that's incongruent. That is not an agreement of parts.

That is inappropriate. When you trade your life for his life, Jesus will give you the power to live right, the power to stand your tests and trials. Jesus does not play favorites. If he sent the power down to Stephen to live right, he can send the power down for you and me to live right.

In the Book of Acts, Stephen called out or exposed some so-called church folk in the synagogue. He was exposing their hypocrisy and they disputed with him. Nor did they like what he had to say to them. The 54th & 55th verses of the 7th chapter say, "When they heard these things, they were cut to the heart, and they gnashed on him with their teeth. But, he being full of the Holy Ghost, looked up steadfastly into heaven, and saw the Glory of God, and Jesus standing on the right hand of God."

Trust me, beloved, if so-called church folk think you are exposing their hypocrisy, they will use their mouths also to hurt you. They will talk about you and lie on you and try to make your life miserable. But do what Stephen did, look up steadfastly into heaven. Behold the glory of God in your life and have faith that Jesus is standing, not sitting, standing, not squatting, but standing on the right hand of God interceding for you. He'll be telling

God to give you more power, to give you more grace, to give you more faith, to give you more understanding, to give you more patience, to give you more courage, to give you more determination, to give you more love as you go through your tests and trials.

As they were stoning Stephen, the Bible says a man named Saul consented unto his death. In today's terminology, he co-signed the stoning of Stephen. He was with that. It was cool with him. He watched the church folks' clothes as they stoned Stephen. He made sure nobody committed the crime of stealing their clothes as he watched an innocent young man being stoned to death. That part was okay with Saul. Kill or imprison all the followers of Jesus, and he tried to, but don't steal these unbelieving church folks' clothes. The Bible says Saul made havoc of the church, entering every house and haling men and women committing them to prison. Think of that beloved, Saul went into every home of whatever town he was, looking to persecute followers of Jesus.

Beloved, if there are some of you reading this who think that your past is too sinful, too dreadful for you ever to be transformed, let me tell you a little more about this sinful, this dreadful man named Saul. One day beloved, this sinful, dreadful, sinister man named Saul was on the road to Damascus to go into every home once he got there to bind all followers of Jesus and take them back to Jerusalem for slaughter. But a wake-up call was waiting on that road and it had Saul's name all over it. Light from heaven shined all around him, and big bad Saul fell to the earth. Beloved, please do not think that because everything is honky-dory, peaches and cream in your life you can't be brought down to your knees.

After he fell, Saul heard a voice saying unto him, "Saul, Saul, why persecutest thou me?" And he said, Who art thou, Lord? And the Lord said, I am Jesus whom thou persecutest: it is hard for thee to kick against the pricks.

Saul knew it was Jesus. He correctly identified him when he asked who art thou, Lord? He knew it was the Lord. I'll tell you something else, beloved, I believe that when Saul witnessed the courage, faith and power that Stephen showed at his death, that it pricked Saul's heart. Jesus began knocking on Saul's heart's door, but that Saul hardened his heart to continue his persecutions. Jesus let him and us know that it is hard to kick against the pricks of your conscience, against the pricks of your heart.

Jesus told a trembling and astonished Saul he was to go into the city and it would be told to him what he must do. Saul obeyed what the Lord told him to do. However, when Saul arose, he was blind. Those that were on the journey with him heard a voice but saw no one. They were on the scene but did not know what was going on. They didn't know where the voice was coming from. Saul was blind for three days. Saul was transformed to Paul. Paul became a champion for Christ.

Beloved, as I close, many people often ask what the meaning of life is? or What are the keys to life? The answer is life is what you make it based on the choices you make. Choices reflect your beliefs. Sometimes we make choices daily that is of little consequence. However, there are also choices we make that are life-altering.

God has offered salvation as a gift through his son, Jesus Christ, to every man, woman, boy, and girl of accountability. We must choose to accept his gift or reject his gift. There is consequence and reward in that choice. I hope you will choose wisely. If you are not saved, I urge you to choose as Joshua did in Joshua 24:15: "...choose you this day whom you will serve...as for me and my house, we will serve the Lord."

If you choose poorly, as the old medieval knight said, and God pricks your heart, remember what Jesus said to Saul, "It is hard to kick against the pricks." The day you hear his voice, like Paul, harden not your heart, but let it be said that you have "chosen wisely".

Vernon & Frances

The Conclusion

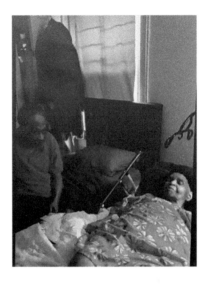

Married for nearly 70 years, September 10, 1950, is when they said, "I do" They exchanged vows promising to stay true. Only a few people were there, including her Mom and Dad, their wedding made the other men who wanted Frances very, very sad.

Vernon and Frances now embarked on a whole new life, she would try her best to be a good housewife. He would work so hard to make ends meet, soon after came the pitter-patter of June's little feet.

Times were hard as their little family grew, it was just a couple years later when little June got a little Bro'. Vernon and Frances looked to God to help them make it through, they now had another mouth to feed, I made little mouth number two.

Divorces were increasing throughout the United States, Vernon and Frances, though, were still true soul mates. Once close families were now being torn apart, not Vernon and Frances, their love was embedded deep in their hearts.

Their marriage was not always, peaches and cream, it was then that on their love and on their Lord, they would more firmly lean. Sometimes the devil would put their marriage under attack, Vernon and Frances refused to put their hand to the plough and then turn back.

They bought a beautiful home on 64th and Langley, here Van was born and welcomed to the family. Frances' parents and good schools were just a short distance away, June and I now had good friends with whom we could play.

My parent's love was never broken only Frances' bones seemed to do that, I am glad she never tripped over Puff, who was our dear beloved cat. Vernon loved to talk about sports, baseball he loved the best, Oh, how he hated it when the Cubs lost to the '69 Mets.

Their love just grew as the years flew by, their love was still strong when we thought that Vernon would die. He was struck by a bullet not meant for him, our life at 64th and Langley suddenly got very, very dim.

Frances stayed at the hospital, rarely leaving his side, she showed love and courage because she was still his bride. God looked down from above on Vernon's devoted wife, because of her love and prayers, God extended his life.

The years have flown by, the children are all grown, June has, and I have grown children of our own. The grandkids and great-grandkids love their "Grandma Sweet and Bay-Bay", we all love them as we celebrate their life and love today.

God has made it possible, in all his wondrous glory, that we are all here to celebrate this amazing, true love story.

They knew that it wasn't always going to be sunshine and blue skies, but what God puts together can't be broken no matter how hard Satan tries.

Van, June, and I owe them such a huge debt of thanks, over the years, we have begged and borrowed more money than is in some banks. But money was not the most valuable thing they gave to us, they gave us love, they taught us to be responsible and they showed us how to trust.

They gave more to us when it meant having less for them, they taught us how to call on the Lord and make him our dear friend. They never blamed each other when things didn't go right, they rebuked the devil when he said, "From this marriage, go, take flight."

Yes, I am proud and thankful for the parents God gave me, to be a good a man as my father, I know I can never be. For Vernon and Frances set the marriage bar quite high, many will never reach it, no matter how hard they try.

Vernon and Frances would not allow death to keep them apart, they passed away within two days of each other, now headed for a brand-new start.

I will miss my parents more than words could ever say, at this funeral, we are celebrating a legacy as we are gathered here today.

So long Mom and Dad, you've earned your wings so bright,
I will see you again when I take my own First Class, eternal
flight.

(Written under God's inspiration on 09/02/20, eight days
before their 70th Wedding Anniversary. Read at their
double funeral service on 09/14/20.)

My Very First

I still cherish my very first look at you, it was a moment that time can never undo. When you were in my arms for that very first embrace, you were also in my heart, in a very, special place.

Through the years, as I have watched you grow, my love for you has reached heights you cannot know. You have grown more beautiful, and smart as a button, now I look around and you are 16, all of a sudden.

You are the firstborn of all my children so loved, and for each of you four, I thank my dear God up above. I hope your special day is filled with laughter and that your wishes come true, while I still reflect on my very first look at you.
Happy Birthday.

(Author's note: This was co-authored with my daughter, Tawanna, who was asked to write a poem for a friend.)

How Can I Live Free from Sin?

Many people today say you can't live free from sin, false preachers have been saying it again and again. Those false preachers have no heaven to put you in, only Jesus has that, so you'd better listen to him.

Jesus said if you die in your sins, where he is you cannot come, don't be deceived, my friend, When life here is over, all is not done. There is an eternity to enter so where will your eternal soul reside, hopefully with Jesus, if in him you forsook the world and did in him abide.

Jesus is light, and there is no darkness in him, Jesus is the Good Shepherd and there is truly no better friend. Jesus laid down his life and became the perfect sacrifice, so we can repent, turn from sin and gain eternal life.

Mankind has created airplanes that keep out oxygen-deprived air, why? So people won't die, choking in utter despair.

Mankind has created great ships to keep out water as it embarks, why? So, people won't be lost and drown or end up swimming with the sharks.

God has created the salvation plan to save a lost mankind that is full of sin, hatred, hardship, and strife, Why? For God so loved the world he gave his only begotten Son, that whosoever believes in him should not perish but have everlasting life.

If man can keep damaging air out the plane and water out the ship, Isn't Jesus powerful enough to keep sin out the heart? Don't you think that God the Father, God the Son, and God the Holy Ghost can cause you to be victorious over sin and make the devil depart?

When Satan presses against you to give up and sin, never forget that by trusting in Jesus, you will always win. So back to the question, "How Can I Live Free from Sin?" The answer is you can't, unless Jesus abides within.

God in heaven will extend you his grace, he is always willing to share, but don't forget that with sin in your life, you won't be entering there.

The Final Warning: Will You Accept or Reject?

Scripture Text: Luke 12:54-56

(54) And he said also to the people, When ye see a cloud rise out of the west, straightway ye say, There cometh a shower, and so it is.

(55) And ye see the south wind blow, ye say, There will be heat; and it cometh to pass.

(56) Ye hypocrites, ye can discern the face of the sky and of the earth; but how is it that ye do not discern this time?

This world has been spinning out of control for some time now. Moral and societal decadence is so low, it is at an all-time high. God has watched sin and decadence prevail in this time more than was in evidence at Sodom and Gomorrah. God destroyed Sodom & Gomorrah for its shameful sinful decadence. He has watched this world become more vile and violent than was in the days of Noah. God destroyed the whole world, saving only Noah and his family. God tries to save before he destroys. God agreed with Abraham that if at least 10 people could be found living right in Sodom & Gomorrah he would not destroy it. Ten people living for God could not be found so only Lot and his two daughters were spared. Lot's wife was spared the destruction of Sodom & Gomorrah, but she disobeyed the commandment given to them not to look back and was turned into a pillar of salt.

Jesus said that the last days would be as it was in the days of Noah. God had Noah preach 120 years to the people of his day. Noah preached as he built the ark beseeching the people to turn from their sins and turn to God. They did not. Despite seeing some things that they had never seen before, things that should have shaken them, they still would not turn to God. They had never seen an ark nor had they ever seen animals coming orderly and peaceably, two by two, onto an ark. Despite those attention-getting sights, they paid God no attention. Instead of looking for mercy, they looked to mock Noah. They believed that since it had never rained from the sky before, there would never be a chance it could happen. It did happen.

God sent the rain down, despite their wayward belief, and flooded the world. God destroyed everything by water, promising that the next time it will be by fire.

Moses gave Pharaoh God's message to let his people go. Moses showed Pharaoh signs and wonders he had never seen before. Pharaoh, however, hardened his heart and refused God. It was not until the death angel came on the scene, the First Passover, that Pharaoh obeyed God and freed God's people. All first-born in Egypt died unless the blood of the lamb, the blood of the sacrifice, was applied to the doors of their dwelling places. Reader, where are you dwelling today? Have you accepted the blood sacrifice of our Lord and Savior, Jesus Christ, as he knocked on your door? Thus, dwelling in the safety of salvation. Or are you dwelling in sin, having rejected that knock on your heart's door? If so, the only way to escape the wrath to come is by applying the blood of the lamb, the blood of Jesus, to your heart's door. Repent of your sins to God and turn away from your sins and allow Christ to make you a new creature where old things are passed away and all things become new.

This world has been at warp speed in rejecting God and the precious gift of salvation by his only begotten son, Jesus Christ. It has been at warp speed in its resolve to eat, drink, and be merry. It has been at warp speed in its course of sin and shame. The sin of this world is a stench in God's nose and who continues to sit and smell a foul stench up their nose? God has smelled the stench of this world for a long time. He is truly longsuffering but everything other than eternity has an expected end; that includes this world. God will soon eliminate that stench, but again, he is trying to save before he destroys in his divine mercy. He tried to get mankind's attention again. God has tried to get mankind to slow down and taste and see that the Lord is good. He has attempted to slow mankind down with Covid-19.

Covid-19 shut down nearly all commerce, industry, education, sports, and socializing world-wide. God slowed down mankind's warp speed of sin down to a "How long before you consider your one eternity bound soul?" type of speed. Mankind has not seemed to want to slow down, so God put an attention-getter in the virus...death. The death tolls have mounted world-wide. What could take the breath away of so many people? The same God who gave the breath to so many people.

Job said in the Bible, "The Lord giveth and the Lord taketh away. Blessed be the name of the Lord." The Bible says that God is not willing that any should perish but come unto repentance. Mankind's sins have separated him from God. God is looking for reconciliation, but it won't be for long. Satan entered into certain government officials and into people worldwide to halt, not the spread of the virus, but to halt trying to interfere with their way of life. They still wanted to frequent the bars, the casinos, the clubs, the strip joints, the theatres, the cannabis shops, etc. They still wanted to do anything and everything that brought pleasure. Everything had nearly come to a halt as God was trying to get people's attention. Some months later, restrictions eased. Government officials bent to the will of the people who were not interested in bending to the will of God.

God has sent a second wave of Covid-19, seemingly deadlier than the first wave, again, for the sake of getting people's attention to alert them they are on their way to a devil's hell if they continue to reject God's Word. However, mankind largely has shown no interest in repentance.

In the Bible, Jonah was sent to Nineveh to warn them that God was about to destroy them for their wickedness. Instead of rejecting the warning, they as a city repented and God did not destroy them.

Now, mankind, in his cleverness, has developed vaccines to eliminate Covid-19. That is an excellent scientific and medical breakthrough, but it bodes poorly for many spiritual breakthroughs to follow. Mankind will lean on the vaccine to get free from the virus, but they won't lean on Jesus to get free from their sins, which is not good.

God will soon say, ladies and gentlemen, that the stench will not go away and that it is time to put it away. Do you not discern this time? Christ is soon to come. God brought something to the world, Covid-19, that has never been seen before, but just like in times past, little-to-no attention has been given to God as he attempts to reach out to a lost and dying world. God has attempted to get the world to pump its brakes, to get its foot off the accelerator of sin. The vaccines will allow mankind to punch that accelerator and go full-throttle back into sin and decay. If God allows full-throttle to resume and do nothing about it, then what would have been the need for a society-slowing, attention-getting, death-dealing virus?

He will do something about it. He will send his Son to render judgment to all. No one will escape that day. I am reminded of how Moses went up into the mountain and was gone such a long time that the children of Israel felt he was not coming back. So, what did they do? They partied and worshipped idols giving no thought to God who had richly blessed them. So, what did God do? He told Moses, "Get thee down for the people have corrupted themselves." Moses returned to the surprise of the people. Moses then separated those who were on God's side and those who were not. The pits of hell then swallowed up those who had rejected God. So, when Jesus returns to the surprise of people doing just what the children of Israel were doing, if not worse, he will have his angels separate those who accepted Jesus and those who did not. Those who did not will be cast into the lake of fire for eternity. Those who did repent and follow him will be with him, pain-free, worry-free, tears-free, temptation-free, disease-free, distress-free, sickness-free, sorrow-free, labor-free for eternity.

In closing, have you seen what the Covid-19 germ looks like? Maybe you saw it on TV or in magazines or on the internet? It is circular shaped with crowns. Ever noticed that many of God's creations: all the planets, the sun, the moon, the eye of a hurricane, and even the ring around Saturn, are all circular. You can't tell where it begins and where it ends. Just like God, no beginning-no end. You could say the circular shape is God's creative signature. What about the crowns? On the last day, Jesus will officially be crowned King of Kings and Lord of Lords, crowned in Glory. Those who are saved will receive their crowns of righteousness and victory. Yes, my friends, Covid-19 has been a sign that God is about to do something. Since man is now on the verge of eliminating the virus from the earth, God is now on the verge of eliminating man from the earth. The earth will then be destroyed by fire and not water as he promised Noah. By two immutable things, the Bible says, God cannot lie.

Nearly everyone has heard that Christ is coming soon. Something you haven't heard is that Christ is coming sooner than that! Will you reject or repent? Please think and choose wisely, but as Jesus told Judas at the Last Supper, "That which thou doest, do quickly!"

About the Author

Vernon L. Coleman has always loved writing and has exhibited that passion even in his Report Writing as an Internal Affairs Investigator for the past eight years. However, he has recently embarked on a new journey as an author. Writing a poetry book was never on his bucket list, but after hearing the voice of God, he became inspired to compose poems that would speak directly to the souls of mankind. While "Father…They Know Not What They Do! God's Poetic Reach to a Lost and Dying World" is his first book, he plans to continue to inspire others as an author by writing other books as God gives him the vision to help promote the Word of God. Vernon says that "choices reflect beliefs" and he chose to listen and obey God's voice to show that he truly does believe in Him.

When Vernon is not writing, he enjoys being with his family, sports, chess, and reading. He currently lives in Illinois and plans to release his next book in the summer or fall of 2021. For more information about Vernon L. Coleman please visit www.vernonlcoleman.com.

CPSIA information can be obtained
at www.ICGtesting.com
Printed in the USA
LVHW071425120421
684234LV00049B/4291